Emotions of Man

THEO WILKERSON

Emotions of Man
All Rights Reserved.
Copyright © 2019 Theo Wilkerson
v1.0

This is a work of fiction. The events and characters described herein are imaginary and are not intended to refer to specific places or living persons. The opinions expressed in this manuscript are solely the opinions of the author and do not represent the opinions or thoughts of the publisher. The author has represented and warranted full ownership and/or legal right to publish all the materials in this book.

This book may not be reproduced, transmitted, or stored in whole or in part by any means, including graphic, electronic, or mechanical without the express written consent of the publisher except in the case of brief quotations embodied in critical articles and reviews.

NGenious Minds

ISBN: 978-0-578-21606-5

Cover by Theo Wilkerson. All rights reserved - used with permission.

PRINTED IN THE UNITED STATES OF AMERICA

Table of Contents

I. Life Lessons
1. Poetic Freestyle (Lyrics) 1
2. The System 2
3. Crack Rock, Jumpshot 4
4. Write my way out 6
5. F!@# The Government 7
6. Poor Richmond 8
7. I Dream Free 10
8. Broken Hour Glass 12
9. Black History 13
10. Freedom of Speech 14
11. Sociological generations (differences) 16
12. Negrartistry (Negro Artistry) 18
13. Real Truth 20
14. Dear Government 22
15. Urban Struggle 23
16. Only in America 24
17. Hashtag #Black America 26
18. Sugarwater (Ghetto Livin') 28

II. Inspired by: Love and other drugs
1. Will I ever 33
2. Done Crying (I'm Sorry) 34
3. Temptations of Man 36
4. I Will Remember you 37
5. Conversation 38
6. A Lover's Essay 40
7. Pheromone Aroma 41
8. Queen Earth (Moms dedication) 42
9. Dear Sister (Dedication) 44
10. White Noise 46

11. I think I might... 47
12. I Made Love 2 U.. 48
13. November 4th 2008 49
14. Ms. Flashing Lights.. 50
15. A Thugs Prayer 51
16. Humble Me..52
17. Definition Of A Woman 53
18. Grown Man (The Growth) 54
19. Heard it all before (A man's plea).............................55
20. Heard It All Before (Male version) 56
21. Through My Eyes 58
22. Spoken Word...59
23. Dear You 60

III. Inspired by The Orgasm

1. Alphabet Love..65
2. Let's talk about Sex...66
3. Love Experience..67
4. Director...Starring You 68
5. Everyday Memory 70
6. An Everyday Memory...71
7. Orgasm...72
8. Cunnilingus..73
9. About Last Night...74
10. The Session..75
11. The Head Doctor (For the Fellas) 76
12. Tongue n the panties 77
13. Teasing me...78
14. Sexual Voodoo..80
15. Explicit Nature..81
16. XXXPlictly You.... 82

Life Lessons

Poetic Freestyle (Lyrics)

Some people sing, rap or dance. I write
Then speak my lyrics into the mic
Bringing truth to light on a dark night when with two brothers lost
I evolve
Then revolve and resolve what I originally thought to be a problem
My addiction to bad karma got me living with daily drama
Like baby mommas, money problems, work to play the starring
role of Batman but end up as Robin. So, he's the man on the block
well I'm going rob'em
Then move to a new city
I want to work for Diddy but, the government's pity got me
collecting checks once a month in this new age recession
Forever stressing, on the verge of becoming a manic depressant
Sex game going downhill because I can't afford a gallon of gas so I
can only get with you if you're willing to do a blockbuster night
With that combo let me get a discount, drink water instead of sprite
trying to save a dollar
My adolescence deprived because I chose to grow up to early in
the projects
That's what we appear to be a project; test to see if we can survive
so for those of you that can feel this hold your hands and heads up
high
We gon make it!!!
Proud of my generation and culture though I lack the knowledge
pass Martin Luther
Now I'm screaming Obama it's time for a change!!!
That's enough for now….

The System

There's a system inside the system.
We are design flaws, expected to fail.
Raised in the projects, a poverty-stricken experiment.
A Living hell this is to keep us in check. Key word keep
The ultimate scheme keep us in debt, no financial freedom.
Give you government support, you think free thoughts yet, you're still systematically in need.
See the cycle.
13th amendment written to imprison and remove civil liberties no citizen but revisited ways of slavery.
Look around at the comparison our blocks flooded with liquor stores and trap houses imported goods, we catch the charge but who owns the boat docks.
Strategically infest low income housing with a way to get out, distribute this dope as hope but, don't cross county lines we will come to you.
See they gave us free but, never land to feed on, a lack of education had us premeditated as robbers to get our eat on.
Slavery still exist if you watching just transformed…. into prison, just look at the numbers if not locked up brown skin turn to victims
Sound of the police no longer a safe haven if your skin is melinated
Our sentence for being called "niggers" is different charged as third time offenders with less than a half. This is to keep the house leaning in their direction cause you are now felon Your voice goes unheard they say you are a No voting nugga, we gave you that as a privilege. You fucked it up, but you had little to no choice.
School system got a test in third grade to determine your direction. As for the others we will simply make them feel like they are not part of the decision, and it's that failed execution; the reason we losing, That's the real trap house

Gave you a figure head, cause they heard you tired of working for the man, the next genius part of plan tarnish the legacy,
Notice how just before the switch of Presidential seat theirs an increase the brutality by police, make it his fault, they winning right now call it off.
Give them the entertainment that's what they seek and spark a twitter beef,
Your whole Presidential tour goal hate is to hate on your predecessor destroy all his credibility.
Don't worry them niggas be often distracted by likes and double taps.
#Fakenews, Instagram models and twitter beef
Gave them access for progress on purpose while also, increasing the diagnosis of ADD
So they attention span is weak; easily diverted we'll sneak
Selfish society claim they woke but refuse to lend their insight.
Keep them trapped in the system, use a revolving door technique let a few escape make believe Illuminati that's too deep
They'll stop seeking knowledge, take the fathers out the community
Preach sexual freedom, even legalize weed
Black lives matter, we like the theme
Trapped in a System within system
Give us, Us Free!!!

Crack Rock, Jumpshot

Its just me, myself and this pen.
Lonely room giving my life to the lines of this notebook, diary quotes. my sweet revenge for the white noise going off in my head. My pen stabilizes the madness, releases me from my rubber room and straight jacket.
The chit chatter has become laughter, my sins have become my blessings.
I am king, born of a royal blood and though I've walked this earth with the scars of my descendants, I carry no grudge for God is the only judge. I've learned overtime, now slavery is understood and I forgive the masters. They were simply trying to get ahead and America well gave them that edge.
Unfortunately based off the color of my skin I only received partial freedom, but no land after farming and giving birth to the economy my families starving,
Now as a man how do I provide, it's that question that's transcended generations Big said
"Either you selling crack rock or you got a wicked jump shot." Or a least that's what they want you to think, when the secrets to the success were well hidden within the ink.
Assumption from the system is that nuggas just learned to read still yet they don't comprehend.
Years later still trying to control our movements using the theories from Willie Lynch.
The social injustice got us taking a knee, backlash is unemployment by 32 teams, point taken now take that shit to the Canadian league your skills no longer fit a NFL scheme but, damn I was just in the Superbowl yesterday... Oh I get it, I must pay for my decision to exercise my first amendment.....
Either you selling crack rock or you got a wicked jump shot."

Until you don't now the brick layer is baking quarter pounds and halves Following the outlined path, that multiplies the math but, divides the family tree now the only way they know dad is behind the glass can't even touch his hand. Now the next generation is like Momma fuck that man! He wasn't there
See the hustle out of the struggle was always in my cookbook; Raised in the trap and pre-judged for my skin color; I'm a menace but what about the European brother that's shooting schools up. Either you selling crack rock or you got a wicked jump shot." Limit my choices athletes or the streets, took away my father figures now I look up to grown adults that look like me, got me thinking rich is solely materialistic. The tradition after over 400 years in an oppressed system and I can barely swim no pools in the hood so where did the drugs and guns that flood my blocks come from?
Image is everything..so either you selling crack rock or you got a wicked jump shot.

Write my way out

Electricity is known to take the path of least resistance
So rather than talk it, my pen transcribes my feelings.
I had to write my way out.
My jump shot was off and now I'm too old to be ducking the laws, crack vials hiding in my drawers me appearing nervous when they stop me for probable cause.
I had to write my way out cuz these days there is an established culture of violence.
Guns delivered to the doors of a Mental asylum. What's your expectation, mass shootings for them coupled by our mass incarceration.
The system is crazy, iron-built plantation the foundation that the US was made on was credited to Slavery. So much white noise surrounding, that rooftop penmanship is sanity. An amazing view I had to write my way out. Be a visionary and see through illusion, crafting my movement in a room filled with people that are my amusement. They want me to lose it; Am I the only one in tune with the music, do they not hear the same sounds, fake news, distracting the neighborhood views. Twitter Pounds hide the real sociological misuse, their dependent on short attention spans, the 24 hour move on.
Police Brutality on the rise, melanin is disguised under hoods as violent, like they want my demise ironic, those that despise they wear hoods to claim and claim a liberal view...
I had to write my way out.
Use my composition as a prescription, when the use of pharmaceutical drugs for mental health are so prevalent.
My motivation is the dictation of my thoughts
Though they remind me my skin is my sin it's also a blend of one part king, one part warrior and one part slave my pen is my weapon brain is fully loaded with the ammunition consumed by the ambition to bear witness to change.
I had to write my way out.

F!@# The Government

You heard me, I said it fuck the government trying to hold me down
Who are you to judge me just because instead of a shirt and tie;
9 to 5 I choose to stand on this corner during the shadows of day and sling dope to fiends.
Fuck makes you better than me,
Fuck gives you the power to be my judge. It is partly my peoples' vote that put you there now you turn around and do this shit to me.
Fucking liars, backstabbers, Labeling me a nigga, a threat to society, some sort of killer. Taking away a system saying it's our abuse and go get a job.
When I tried that no matter my qualifications I'm turned down because I braid my hair and wear baggy clothes.
So I figured that's not my role you don't want me there I do what you do cheat and lie to get by.
Does that make me a bad person. Enemy of the state.
Corrupt bastards cheating the hoods man.
Making it hard for a black man already struggling everytime I turn around taxes up, rent done raised and you wonder why I do what I do.
You got us cornered, back against the wall. Shit I gotta eat to.
So label me what ya'll want, lock me in your cells, hope we kill each other off we'll see you rat bastards in hell.
Understand though Mr. President, governor, senator, and mayors no matter the outcome we will survive and at least we won't get caught up in your millennium slavery master plan fuckers.
Let my people go."

Poor Richmond

You place me in the projects
As if I'm a project
And expect my voice not to project
But, I detest regression
Manifest progression from the 8th Section
Where nine millimeters and other heaters are protection because police just don't come around
Can't get a delivery after dark and public parks get shut down,
Fuck am I supposed to do now
We live in the village of the damned
A place where dreams diminish, we're looked upon as sociological menace
Single parent homes where moms is strung out and pops is a rolling stone
Could've been the next Michael Jordan but, the boy couldn't leave the corner alone
And look over there at America's next top model
Yet, other than the club she ain't taking pictures too busy fucking around with them bring her down constitutants. Now half way through high school she's the mother of 2
See the neighborhood I'm from is full of legalized prostitutes
That's what the Government do
Inport it through, sell it to the slums
Keep us in low paying jobs so we either sell dope, get high to cope or steal and rob to get by
It's a ploy to destroy us
Heads up people we gotta make better choices And Be For Us
Educate ourselves and become the lawyers
Flip that 9 to 5 and become the employer's employer
U a hustler ain't it then show em change

How we can come from that beaten down Buick to the 09 Range
Be OUTRAGED!! Then go INSANE and AMAZE
They don't want you to win
Rather zoo us, that's what they do lock animals in and watch from a distance
But, don't feed the animals let them fend for themselves
The place I speak of is my home I love "Poor Richmond"
The Capital City of Virginia
Picture that!

Dedicated to: Every state, city or town where the government denies your existence be heard!

I Dream Free....

"I HAVE A DREAM THAT ONE DAY THIS NATION WILL RISE UP AND LIVE OUT THE TRUE MEANING OF its CREED:"
"WE HOLD THESE TRUTHS TO BE SELF-EVIDENT, THAT ALL MEN ARE CREATED EQUAL."
I dream that in the future their will be no blacks, whites, or Mexicans
Skin will be transparent, race is see through
I dream of a nation that will be free from violence and racial teachings
Where we as Americans can walk the street without peeking getting nervous at the other color and reaching
A nation free from its horrid history
Father forgive me as I walk upon this blood stained slave soil, a country built off free labor that's become freedom's misery
I dream a free dream of a country where a dollar makes a dream not turn a once promising prom queen into a crack fiend
A nation that is drug-free
An America where money is not the root of all evil and poverty and disparity doesn't exist
"WHERE MY KIDS AND THEIR KIDS WILL BE JUDGED NOT BY THE COLOR OF THEIR SKIN BUT, BY THEIR CHARACTER'S CONTENT"
It is evident and apparent that our nation still suffers
He can't be my brother because of his skin color
Then she suffers as a single mother
Police thought he fit the description of another
Racial struggle took her lover
100 years past a King's dream; we still dream today

His held at a podium in Washington DC, mines on the streets of Richmond, VA
Let's come together as a nation
Put away the whips, chains and nooses that hang
Rid ourselves of the colored rags that represent us as a gang
Let's all hold hands, join as one ring to represent the now generation in prayer to save the future generation
Bow our heads and speak the closing words of MLK as if it were an incantation
"FREE AT LAST, FREE AT LAST, THANK GOD ALMIGHTY WE ARE FREE AT LAST."
Let's escape our past and live for our future
I dream free…….

Broken Hour Glass

Am I trapped or is there an escape?
Should I live in doubt as if I won't succeed.
Cut my wrist and watch it bleed, then will I continue to breath on earth as it is in heaven or will I even see that pearly gate, my fate is doomed concealed within my hands lacking guidance because I don't seek it.
Am I scared to greet it or is it the reality we live in that has me blinded.
Where is the light? How does it shine in all this darkness….
failure is upon us what have I done that is so wrong placing myself through torture, battered legs and bruised arms, they say remain calm and it will come in due time…But time is a deception of the mind, A young man's future, yet a dying man's past it's also fragile, and if not careful you'll break the glass…So I ask myself will I last?

Black History...

I am black history, just Look at me
Through my veins runs the blood of my ancestral slaves
That same blood is also from kings and queens making me
One part slave; one part royalty
Brought from my African homeland
To build another land; then told that I am the lesser man
Because of the color of my skin
That same skin that has been scorched by the sun's rays
Lashes on my back because I didn't obey what you say
Understand that I am black history
My struggle, comes from a slave driven misery to a freedom land
I am Original man, Scientifically proven
At the Olympics I held high one black fisted hand in victory
I do not seek sympathy; only build from the seeds planted in my memory
My forefathers were a part of suffrage, embezzlement from another continent
Years later there is still no settlement
Can't depend on a lawyer or the government
They are the same people that enslaved me in the first place
So what I did was fight, bite, scratch with the spirit of Kunta Kinta
and scream "Give us us free" like Sin-Kay and with Ms. Tubman's assistance via the Underground Railroad made my escape
Now that same plantation where my descendants were beaten, raped and portrayed as slaves while they roamed, I bought the land now I own
Where I was not allowed the freedom to speak in a normal tone
I speak now with a microphone in front of crowds
My physical was beaten down in history; that only makes me stronger now
Those before me practiced starvation; I now feed my hunger
America is dependent upon my dollar for its very existence
That's why I live everyday like its Christmas
Damn, we came a long way from being Nigga boys and wenches
I am black history…each and everything that happened before me is part of me
My bloodline…

Freedom of Speech...

Through mental exercises
I prophesize some of the hottest lines of my generation
Who am I; doesn't matter
As long as when I speak I apply enough matter to create an optical shatter
So if you wear glasses or have fragile ears you need to move to the back
Scratch that as a matter of fact switch states because I contemplate thoughts with the complex mental state of 200 genius men
Me and my pen sentenced to lifetime bids for our creativity
My plea
It's not me your honor that's guilty blame God he blessed me with this ability
Silly me for thinking that a black man had a chance in this judicial system
They'd rather lock me away for the minimum
Than to let me walk away Scott free with my innocence
So with that being said it is my intent to spit the truth, the whole truth
Whether or not you like or believe it; now that I totally up to you
Because I have the freedom of speech
I am only one man so I can only speak about what I hear, witness or see
And what I see is my city is a travesty
Under funded school systems leading to the youths miseducation
Drugs imported, then sold leading to crack babies and probation
Under developed housing projects
Pops got mom pregnant, then pop decides to jet leaving an innocent child questioning "Where's my daddy at?"
These sights spark the flame inside of my soul to bless the pad then recite to the mic

I watch my people being robbed and shot from my window at night
And who gives a fuck about my poverty?
 I do obviously; that's why my speech is deep because I want to free
Give me a piece of American pie take these fucking chains off me
So if I offend you with what I've been through
Good that means your heart or at least mind was touched
So if you're that judge that wants to lock me up
So what I'm not trying to be hard but, I don't give a fuck
My job is done.

Sociological generations (differences)

We were the dealers,
They became the users.
We had library books they, do it all from computers.
We screamed fuck the police
Now 911 are the abusers.
Their fashion sense is more sensitive than ours
They wear longer shear shirts we came up in the durags and timberlands environment.
We were gentleman, they're much more aggressive
We fought after school they run home and jump on Twitter.
Our hip hop had bars, words put together with a defined meaning
Theirs are melodic and they can say whatever, Same talent just a different level.
Promoting prescription drug abuse, which is funny when the government is now trying to take access to medication from the youth
We the people are evolving some for the better, to old heads seem as if the generation didn't get the message but it took us 30 years to move past the Reagan era...when Clinton started taking our stars away for dealing methods, investing in prisons and we adopted his efforts as the first black president
I mean we never thought we would really see it.
Ironic how, 2008 you were raised in a generation to see son.
We grew up hard workers,
They are the lucid dreamers, As our offspring they have inherited our demons.
We use to wish it was and easier way
Now, they can WWW. Their life away and gain access to know information
Can it be all so simple, so not knowing something is no longer the fault of the school system but, you now play your own victim.

It used to take a village to raise, now half the village are the villains. So time no longer spent assisted in raising and developing children but watching the who's who's.
Reality tv now in a neighborhood near you.
Its now a Sociological norm that men are born women, open acceptance when we hid these activities in closets.
Gay or Bi there was no difference now there is the softer terms of pseudosexual.
Open transgender winning track competitions should've seen it coming, we mad but, why a trophy goes to everyone.
Championship winner, the MVP and basic play look the same way.
Competition slowly going missing from the game.
Jordan was the GOAT based off Championship Rings, Lebron the GOAT now but, the basis has changed and the Mamba Kobe no one mentions the name.
Rap has turned RnB.
Cuz ghost writing is accepted as long as your shit comes off fire, it's okay to hire.
Sure, it's been there but, now they want the credit.
See it was written that your children shall not suffer for the sins of their father, The offspring inherited the demons.
Generations.

Negrartistry (Negro Artistry)

Born into a concrete plantation,
Seeking the education needed for mind elevation,
Segregation is our downfall, nah, it's just an excuse to do less.
A word that raised our youth. our forefathers fought so we could be free but, i gaze thru shaded Windows only to see brothers living in slavery. not in the physical but, in a mental state.
Using poverty as the word that seals our fate but, there is an escape cause we as children really have no Idea what poverty is, compare yourself to your parents bro and you'll see that we're rich kids.
So fuck doing bids and rocking afro wigs believe me man that shit ain't cool, you'd be a damn fool not to use that god given tool that blesses you,
Excel your mind they can't take that, anything they do take, use your mind and take it back…that'll hurt more
Now realize that it's a blessing to be black of an afro American descent, and even though it makes the world go around don't be possessed by those dead presidents.
Taking to the streets for your residence when you should be fathering your child instead, take a look around and bear witness to the truthful evidence, the living definition of black on black crime, we killing ourselves, hating on each other and still we blaming them as you call them "those white muthafuckas"
Why should you suffer screaming drugs is the only thing that gets you by, when what it really does is give you a high, so you can fantasize about your true reality.
Black man drugs are the root to our sin, so then why sell it to our people, or smoke it with your people that damn sho isn't the way to become equal, just a slave but, now in different trade.
Now look at your skins' shade isn't it beautiful man? If you agree then

Ask yourself this question why settle the score by beating on and calling our women "bitches and whores"
She was placed here for you as one of Gods' greatest creations c'mon my brothers.
Let's start the separation to give us liberation from this stereotype.. the black man is God. especially when he uses his mind right… you with me????!!!

Real Truth

A floating prison, Voluntary slavery
Disillusioned lies advertised for the love of your country and bravery
Trains you to be a killer, brainwashes the mind to make you believe that they are the villain and the Wonderful United States of America and her precious liberty you're defending
Yet, the neighborhood you were raised in is in a penniless state
Electoral debates both parties claim to relate to the minorities yet cater to the majorities
Because 2,4,6,8 years go by and you still ignore me. Nothing you claim happens
Still at night outside my window pane there's that familiar sound of guns clapping, and drug trafficking's a secret government organized crime covered up by it's over emphasis in the black community to the public.
Their plan is import it, let the minorities sell it
Kill two birds with one stone crack down on crime, snatch the money and balance the budget
You gotta be kidding me; The government corrupt in the land of the free
The Master manipulators with society under its lock and key
They teach segregation through education, profile races hidden all in equal opportunity documentation and we sign off on it
Thinking it's something that helps, That it's there for us
Truth be told All of us are lost, not just one
Organizations, underpay us
Corporate America reaches her quota then she begins to hate us
Who can we trust ? When prison is the only place that will gladly accept our applications
They're scared of us because, to our struggle there's not relating

We either hustle, ball or bust
They looking to make a big name a statistic before the rich nigga looks beyond the materialistic
See the true lies of our system and use his corporate power and wisdom to start a revolution
That rewrites our beloved constitution then our plans are ruined. That's the real truth.

Dear Government...

I speak for the voiceless people
Those with a skin hue of a dark transparency
The invisible man that can't be seen
This is our testimony
Dear government remember me
It was my vote cast that voted you in
My tax dollar that got you that pearl white benz
What did I receive in return
Nothing
Views ignored left in hell to burn
While you hold an ash less Hearn because I couldn't afford to be buried
Constantly pulling me over when I cannot afford the lawyer fees
Tease me with street dreams; then lock me away and throw away the key
My dreams now are the day that I'm freed from the concrete walls and iron bars of the penitentiary
For 400 years we endured this, and you still put me through this
No this is not a sob story looking for a handout
Just want a chance to get my hand out and break away from the cycle of this poverty chain
Minimum wage saved trying to get the next generation out of this trap
We're waiting in a long line outside your door attempting to knock
Yet scared for your life you keep door locked. HEAR US CRY!

Urban Struggle

I try to do right but, you steer me in the wrong direction
I come to you seeking help, yet you seek your own protection
You say I lack education but, refuse to teach me
I place my hand out for your guidance but, you don't attempt to reach me, just turn your back on me and continue to let me starve. Not realizing that i could have been the next Kareem-Abdul Jabbar, now a nigga gotta eat.
So should I take a one in a million shot at the NBA or invest in some heat, cop a new jeep and take a trip out of town once every 3 weeks.
Let me think seriously
I looked for your help and you didn't want to be bothered and now I got a seed which results into another problem. Two mouths to feed
I guess you know my choice. no doubt indeed, the streets are my destination and if I have to endure the consequences and do a bid locked away and in trouble, it'll still be safer than being caught up in these infested streets known as the urban struggle.

Only in America...

See only in America can I be found guilty for distribution and using, when my Uncle is the one abusing
See ya'll I got an uncle named Sam that raised me crazy and I'm finding out he's a hypocrite
He imports the shit, I bag then sell it for a profit
Then Bobby Blue Note raids my house to lock me away for distribution
Now that's confusing looking at the Economy
Where I'm from that's how you make it hustle, rap, water jump shot or sing
I'm in a neighborhood full of abusers, diminished dreams and no one is pursuing their goals
We're raised to be insignificant, arm tied heroin addictions
Vote for a politician that claims a change but, Sam Cooke never comes around my way
I pray for an escape; Grandma says continue on baby and they'll come true one day
I Never wanted to be born a bastard...But, Daddy went away
So, I'm raised from the theatrics of Belly, Shottas and Scarface
So, what's my race place, our sociological purpose
Play ball, cook, smoke and sell to the worthless tricked by society like we on some recycle the earth shit and Thugs now in days are no more than struggling actors
Pretending to be hard, Sling rocks on the Boulevard
Then dry snitch to reduce the charge; That ain't gangsta at all
See only in America can one race be prostituted and still have the biggest influence on elections
Americans are extorted due to our tax bracket; upper class get the break, lower half gotta pay
He who owns the land, owns the man this country has been that way

That's why back in the day there were slaves. Cheap Labor and Liberty that's how we built this land of opportunity. Secretly maybe the definition of a democracy
Where else can you go from racial friction, to determining what love is because the couples gay.
Are we really free? Richest country in the world still in debt
Go figure that
Then come back and tell me why you can be successful doing some crooked shit.
 Only in America!!!

Hashtag #Black America

To hell with average, I want to be amazing
Duegard sign, Holy Bible, Compass and square I'm a Mason
Not saying I'm a mason but, I want to be at the table engaged in decision making conversations,
Discussions about my future
The Government is corrupt, ran by lucifer
Asphyxiation I can't breathe Officer, what did you do that for I wasn't reaching for a gun
You asked me for ID
Claim to fear me because of my skin tone, when history says I'm the beginning of man
Yet I'm resisting arrest, handcuffed and shot in back, day before my marriage 50 times I got hit
Told I'm a thug because of my hooded head and there's no question asked if you think I'm reaching, you shooting first. How is this policing, Protecting to serve but, your piece leaves me deceased
Am I just an easy target when it's 42 percent them 19 percent me carrying an open piece
Racial profiling me when a group named ISIS is wilding claiming every unfortunate opportunity
When have you known a black man to have terrorist tendencies. See our grandfathers had to run, we walking our generation is out of breath we ain't running no more Stokely Carmichael quotes as we grabbing rifles
We protest, but we protect our families with vest ; Lack of trust you don't trust me so there's no trust from us When I dial 9-1-1 for hood conflicts you take your time to show up
My family went from 10 toes down to 10 toes up fuck!
More tears shed at another funeral, I need to stop this trend

Government won't help so I'm not thinking congressman I'm leaning towards a revolutionary end
I see that black gloved fist going up again, beret caps, black shades, black sweater men but wait if History repeats itself then we on track for slavery again so now black America
I'm speaking to you we are raising our youth not to respect authority figures
Teach them to say sir/ ma'am to them and do away with the word nigga
We say black lives matter but I swear that's just a cover up because right now we helping them kill us
Then pleading that we the victims, no passes given, we sissified now
Stop fist fighting, we picking up guns and shooting our brethren
How the fuck is that helping, like we never learned our lessons
Please my people recall those Willie Lynch letters
The system was built against us
Using Distrust and hatred, placing the old vs young, man vs the woman , put that dark skinned melanin against that light skin one
Make it quick, give him a gun
See the Second amendment gives you the right to bear arms, I'm thinking like them
They'll raise a nation of punks and do the work we wanted done slide their neighborhood drugs they'll either take it or sell it either way we'll make a killing get it
but, brethren remain calm "Know thyself, know thy enemy, 1000 battles, 1000 victories"
The Art Of War given in a book to me
So be peaceful, be courteous and respect everyone as we pray for Peace Love and unity
Hashtag #Black America

Sugarwater (Ghetto Livin')....

Funny, how we had so much fun being broke
Playing ghetto games to stay entertained not the Playstation things
Pretending like we were things we really ain't
Screaming out that's my car but, couldn't afford it
Drinking juice out of an old pickle jar
Out of Kool-aid so we drank Sugar Water
We didn't need a waterpark
We had the slip n' slide with the Fire Hydrant on the corner
We kept popping that
Mr. Police man would come round and say we were jeopardizing the cities water
We give a fuck though
We could get icebergs for a quarter
You remember
Candy lady sold pickles and skittles
Damn it was so easy being little
Remember Mr. Softee, everything you were doing stopped
Out the house in full sprint, bare foot
Chasing the ice cream truck with a buck to buy a bomb pop
Skipping school because we accidentally on purpose set our alarm clock for 6pm
To miss the bus, sometimes just to catch a ride and mom or pops woke up mad as fuck
Gotta love that ghetto living; not that I'm trying to go back I'm just reminiscing on how much I enjoyed that feeling you got from having a crush on your babysitter
Playing K-I-S-S-I-N-G in the tree with your boy's sister
So innocent, so sweet it like a cold glass of sugar water
What you know about helping your mom take clothes to the laundry mat
Trouble again!

Pick a switch, the smallest you can find and say what's wrong with that
Whole time grandma already got one just waiting on you to come back
We use get beat black n' blue
I'm talking beatings from moms, pops, and the neighbor too
Younger siblings snitching AW! You trouble, not knowing for telling they in trouble too
Them were the days
Growing up we didn't have much, but enjoyed what we had
List of food went something like this
Peanut Butter, Jelly, bologna, hot dogs, pork n beans and spam and of course Sugar Water
Them Saturday Cartoons with a bowl of generic Cap'n Crunch
Going to the Rec center just for some fee lunch
Shooting ball all day, acting like our favorite players from the NBA and we thought all the girls had cooties Shit; all of us were gay….
If you can relate to this then, see you fit the description
Remembering the fun times we never got bored huh well, reminisce with then and toast as we sip from this Sugar Water!

II. Inspired by: Love and other drugs

Will I ever

For you it must be nice, While I decide will I ever fall in love again
The words of a scolded man with his heart in hand
Finding it hard to trust women again; I can only give my heart once and fall in love twice
Yet you tell me I love different, I don't understand
Men are from Mars, Women from Venus yet our hearts beat the same
The same intentions with different visions
Thanks to you though, now women are coincidentally existence is behind iron partisans
No longer a desire for a wife only a mistress,
Ms. Right Now for a man of the moment
Before you retaliate in defense
I just want you to know that you made me this way
All the nights I sat at home and behaved, you contradicted my love as being a runaway
Although at home, in your eyes I was another bitches love slave
So, know my heart pumps nova cane through the veins of a lonely man being blamed
Now framed, Weakness exposed I become enticed by beautiful things
So, what I hit the strip club and spend some change
The only thing I know about Desire is her stage name
Without TRUST our love will never be the same, only going through the motions of romance
Misguided interpretations of what real love is
I provide, not socialize
Deliver deep dick, and a supporting shoulder to cry
Make decisions based off the situations not acting on emotions
I may not have the answers sometimes, but I try
Now injured and heartbroken I may never love again
Staring at the man in the mirror asking God one question
Will I ever love again?
Inspired by: The soul of a man scolded

Done Crying (I'm Sorry)

Baby I'm Sorry, I never meant to hurt you
She never meant shit, I was only flirting
Your Girl called and told me you were hurting and thinking about leaving
Please hear me out before you make your final decisions, I need ya
You're done crying; that's probably an understatement
My pictures today instead of love smiles, probably bring on a sensation of hatred
I messed up baby, okay I'm man enough to say it
Now please give me another chance to dance the sweet romance as your man
Don't leave me outside in the cold, I'm lost without you
Just a lonely soul roaming without a destination
A wandering man, needing to be loved naked
The famous words of a lonely man I'm sorry, forgive me baby
I know I got a history of heartbreak that's just my mischievous behavior in fear of exposing my deepest feelings, trying not to expose my heart to the possibility of being staken as if I'm a vampire
My deepest desires are only to love you
Harder and stronger than I did yesterday, but I need help baby
I need fulfillment from the temptation
The world is filled with witches I need to know that you are that perfect lady for me
Perfect not is the sense of perfection but, in the sense of the errors of your ways for I am not perfect only a man as Adam was to Eve
U remember you told me love me; and I told you the same thing those feelings haven't changed
Been abducted by alien beings but, that's because neither of us were on our game
We play the post not the perimeter baby, execute a pick and roll

Please don't leave not now baby
I'll stop breathing without you, heart will stop beating cardiac arrest without you
You are my CPR, my medication to keep down my heart rate.
I can only say I love you so many ways, but if you take me back
I'll say just that as a reminder every day
I love you 24/7 365 days.

Temptations of Man...

At times I wish I was blind so that I could see life's true identity
I got a loving wife at home, yet I love to chase that pretty, brown round bootie
I got a problem with women, I just like to damn many There's Rhonda, Tanisha, Rebecca and Penny.
Never to my family do I mean any harm
I thought I was just a man it's hard living with regrets, Hate the fact that I'm a dog, don't mean to be wrong, making mistakes like having another woman in my arms
I guess they're simply turned on by my innocent charm
Don't want a relationship prior to conversation we establish this
And I originally had no intent of hitting her off Ridiculous
I never mean for a friendship to go to far but, I'm a man exposed to have a weak soul
I pray, listen attentively to what the preacher preach and I study the words that the bible speaks
Yet a peek at an hour glass physique and theirs images of adultery
So, you see lord I need you to work with me. Strengthen my soul as you do my body.
For the flesh of a man is weak
Help me to fight off the temptations that's bringing me farther from my home you oh lord and closer to satan, My wife you gave unto me to be my queen, give birth to my princess
God knows that my lil man that's my heart
Can't say enough about my family in each sentence
So guide me lord and in your footsteps I'll willing follow
So in this marriage I will do right and not become alone, empty and hollow
AMEN!

I Will Remember you

I'll remember her beyond her beauty; With my inquisitive mind
Though I never really had that one on one time to expand on her inner design
And structure; I'll tell her now
I desperately wanted her
Taunted with her imagery in a nocturnal state so that I could go to sleep early and wake up late
I resisted the temptation ; Kept telling myself that she was already taken; Simply awaiting
Time spent wasted who knows what this could have been
Erotic Stimulation to coincide with her voice, and seductive scent of succulence
Although bent I resisted the temptation to pursue and simply toyed with thoughts in my imagination
She was born of a matrix
Her appearance an elegant caramel complexioned queen
Sitting in my room with a clear view just staring for hours I could just watch
I'll remember her for her pursuit and drive for excellence and pray for her happiness as I pray for mines
Time…tick, tick away
I'll miss you and remember her none other than a fitting place for her to be found other than
Queens…..

Conversation

Let's have a conversation about conversation
Since it's the foundation, let's build a solid structure; plants seeds well nurtured
I wanna role play as your BFF, boyfriend., Husband and moonlight as your lover
All rolled up in one
Right ear hears I love you boo, left ear hears damn I hate him! Child Please
I wanna go from exotic body language vacations on the island of exctasy to sipping Mai Tai's poolside off the Imafi Coast engaging in intriguing conversations about everything and nothing
Chaperone you to a Gentleman's affair; escort you to ladies night where you're unaware of my presence there as your naught inhibitions come to life and you purchase your battery operated boyfriend so that when I'm not around you can pretend with the help of seductive images and your rabbit
Rather than be jealous; I might use it the next time we're stuck in traffic to get you off
See trust starts before the clothes come off
Whispers of the emotions of love are hidden, not in saturated lips, interlocked in a forbidden kiss but, stimulated from adjectives, nouns and verbs
So again let's have a conversation about conversation put everything on the dinner table and indulge in a full course meal about each other
This way we leave nothing to chance, either you love me or leave me alone, no secrets, no reason to go in each others phone and wonder who's that and who's this
Responding so immaturely as tossing words like who's this nigga, or who's that bitch by conversations end we ain't shit and there went a perfectly good chance to have a relationship

Therefore, I ask you to trust me like you would your brother and I shall you as I would my own mother at the same time we make love to one another like forbidden lovers
All do to engagement in simple conversations that became the basis of our love affair
Communication is a seed planted that allows prosperity in relations…

A Lover's Essay

I want to be the subject of her conversations about love.
Be her dissertation of the possibility of falling in love,
Be her adjective that specifies real love
Her adverb, noun and predicate of the conversations she's having about her man
Shit, I want to live dangerous and make her friends jealous like "bitch for real again, we talking bout him, he ain't all that"
Yet she secretly wants one
I want to be every other word of her lexicon
The opening paragraph and thesis for her lover's essay
The Body of the conversation and ending paragraph on the subject of some of her best work
I want to reach pinnacles like define a silver anniversary and the family simply looks at us
I want to author chapters together call it "Love like us"
Be in love for no reason, because there's no limitations on us
It's unconditional
That means I have no reason that I love her like I does I simply do
Fucked my grammar up, in hopes that you get the point
I'm fiending to be a hopeless romantic because a hopeless person no longer gives a fuck
But, to get there babe we gotta work
We are not perfect I've been through shit and so have you
Put it all on the table, have a conversation figure it out
The Key word Fight through the bullshit, through the hate and discontent
We gotta commit 100 percent to us
Trust one another and be loyal to a fault
Let the past be the past
Move on, Forgive and Forget
For every bad chapter, we got to stay focused on the precision penning and the goal is a happy ending

Pheromone Aroma

This is my dedication to that intoxicating fragrance that you wear;
An ode to exctasy
Slowly luring me in
See, I started off my morning half-crazy by noon I'm clinically insane and it's all do to that Pheromone Aroma
Each of my steps now misguided as I seem to be drawn to you; following you the wrong way mind saying right but, you pass and my body does a left face; the stalker within released in search of that scent of strawberry molasses, mango honeydew romance
You Smell like the sweetest forbidden fruit; nasal ingestion allows my imagination to taste you
And you taste as good as you smell
So, you forever remain on the tip of my tongue and I continue to water your roots as nourishment
Your fruit juice in place of water such a relaxing aromatherapy
Sensual Seduction in a bottle of chemistry; PH Balanced to perfection to excite the male species
That fragrance makes me lose my mind
As you pass me by I want to snatch you up, pin you up against the wall and release my animalistic intentions,
Tracing your bodies dimensions until I'm face to face with that exotic bubble and use it as my straw to suck out your bad girl inhibitions
I want to bathe in your oils, then bottle you up as a candle and burn it so that when you're away I can still smell you; I want you embedded in the odorous molecules of my cerebellum
Your scent creates temptation and delicate desires
Now I understand a vampire's fascination with fairies' blood; your scent is an emotional high
The sweetest aroma therapy.

Queen Earth (Moms dedication)

She is queen, also known as old earth
She is genetically designed to give birth, she is the definition of love, the nurturer.
She has so many talents, it was from her that I learned how to create a balance. School, home and work.
It's was from her teachings that now I know my worth, though due to gender biases she most often doesn't get what she deserves, still like a seasoned warrior she fights, lack of complaints, with woman we witness true sacrifice, and it was her struggle that taught me what true love was, to identify with the differences between when to be soft and when to be hard.
Moms heart is always with God, he made us first and them second get the lesson our flaws became her perfection. They carry our rib, feed and develop infant kids it's scientifically proven the healthier option is to be breastfed. Pops would beat me off mistake made, moms didn't have the physicality so would mentally challenge me, force me to read books encrypting my mind with the ideologies of right and wrong. Mental exercise led to plans designed to conquer the earth, she taught me how to dream; and put in that work.
See men there is no you without her, the woman's womb is where we found safety first. Comfort in her breast, then as we age its funny how the roles reverse, after birth irony how now our job is to protect her.
Isn't it amazing the way their bodies stretch 9 months new life development, pop out embryo then back to where it left.
For without woman there is No breath, I mean we truly don't exist. Honor thy woman who carried the seed planted, way to often we men scream young and run from the responsibility, "shit I got dreams and can't raise a little me."

Now here's another single parent home, lost and alone she scared but, you'd never know it see moms is a meta human. Able to gain patience from God, find a way when there seemingly isn't none. Belly full, lights on she even found a way to get you some J's on.
She is Queen of the Universe but,I simply call her MOM
Ladies we appreciate and love ya'll!!

Dear Sister (Dedication)

The black women is queen
There is no other like you in existence whether
Dark chocolate, cocoa, or butterscotch skin all with gold and honey blended
Complexion is part of your black excellence
Her melanin skin got a vast gene pool dating back to old earth which is 4.5 billon years of age
The educated authors of the household perfectly sculpting the theme that love over all other things. Just when you think you got away, momma too soft she fucks you up and reminds you she did it out of love
My Sister, Your strength comes from struggle. Underpaid but rarely complain
They were intrigued by your physique, in love with your skin, raped and separated us as slaves, so the broken family was born in those early days Left hopeless so dealing with both race and sexual bias in America didn't prevent you from going corporate You own it.
My Sister,
You profoundly navigate, achieve the highest degrees of education these numbers are statically proven then you motivate your man to pursue dreams start the movement think Coretta Scott to Martin Luther
My sisters
The keepers of those natural curves, got other races like I want hair and figure like hers. I mean That sundress ain't never looked that good. Whether Kinky twist, Caesar fade, braids or a messy bun we're intrigued by her look hoping you have a nice day Mrs. Versatility.
My sister,

When I think of you I think of a divine goddess crafted from rib meaning I may have been first but, in you god placed the perfections from the initial experiment and in return I was given equilibrium.
I think of that black girl magic, educated and established
I think of BAE, as my black and educated sister
Comparing her melanin mixture of Nefertiti, Isis, Omi, Yemaja and Oshun.
I apologize for the added stress at times to the mothers, daughters, aunts
My black sisters I love you!

White Noise

I need this to expose my soul
Prayer knee, quoting bible verses
Gun on my right side, knife to my left
Negotiating terms for my life after death
My last breathe remember was my scream for help.
Pen in my hand at 3am...that's the only time I don't hear noises
Hoping to Make the right choices while posting
Holding guns and money, a big booty snack her ass is dummy
Placed over brilliant verses
So much going on in my head
Alone in this bed yet feel the knife fingered hands pulling me in.
Mind formulating cryptic verses this blessing I'm cursed with
Suicidal tendencies increased from shots of Hennessey
If I die tonight how will they remember me?
Fuck it I don't care anyway all he had to say was hope you are having a good day and he ignored me; That two cuts vertical to vien and artery or should I choose self inflicted gun shot wounds
Would you see me in this cubicle then
What my life like, mind filled with the nonsense
I'm hearing voices angel on my right, devil on my left
Braclet on wrist states what would jesus do
Does he see these demons too HD vision, corrupted mindstate, Altered thoughts of sanity
In relation to medically induced diagnosis pay attention to your surroundings
My intention was not to die tonight but, seek help aloud due tocomplications with my mental health
White noise got me fucking crazy
Dedicated to Mental Health

I think I might...

I think I just might like her, Her conversation is stimulating
She's a bully, do to her life stages
Her success for most men would be intimidating
Yet, I'm prepared to face it, reverse the fear factor we both drop
our guards in a surprising fashion
Asking how the fuck did you get here
I think I just might
After A decade of mental infatuation with the possibility of maybe
I think I might like this awkward situation
Like I find myself intrigued, genuinely interested in things outside
of her body.
Though she is eye candy and a succulent piece
A walking aphrodisiac, sometimes I lose my ability to speak
Her lips taste like passion and her eyes have those bedroom curves,
shit even the formulation of her words like boy stop, you get on my
nerves have me with a laser focus
I'm Turned on and turned out
From here the rabbit hole fall doesn't look that long
The debate is fall, push, pull or jump
Either way we will hold hands and advance.
I think I might like her.

I Made Love 2 U..

Last Night I made love to you
Late for work, had to explain to my boss that I made love to you
Submerged deep within
The bedroom became an exotic island for two
Me, you purple satin sheets, moonlight, a cool summer's breeze
Naked our only clothing the curtains of the canopy bed we rest in
It was there that our physical speech was a painting of Zane's Sex chronicles
There I learned to speak another language
It was that moment, that very minute
That got me round the clock reminiscing
Going through a Mid day De Ja vu
Secret rendezvous
A table set for two surrounded by palm trees and white sands of a beach
Hmmm; that body of yours is a sweet physique
Recipe to bring out the freak in me…I like to eat
Last night I made love to you

November 4th 2008....

The day November 4, 2008
A day to celebrate; on this day we went from shackles and chains
Being called out of our name to standing on a podium, hands raised taking on the oath as Chief executive of the USA
Who would ever believe that we could achieve this moment
Paparazzi snapping pictures of speeches a Time Life Image
While Journalist quoting the phrase "Believe in Change"
Dr. King had a dream
They say dreams only come true in your sleep but, he felt so strongly about his
He was an insomniac and turned his nocturnal vision into a speech of intrigue
After 400 years of oppression, Segregation and skin negligence
With our lucrative economy half way into a recession
We still trying to get our 40 acres and a mule plus still seeking reparations
The strength instilled in our skin complexion
Who better to run this struggling nation than us?
I mean we fought back from whips and chains; being labeled as monkeys, niggas, coons and slaves
Now we seeing and our kids, kids can see what happens with hard work, dedication and patience
We didn't come this far to paint the White House black we merely to cast a shadow 44x4, 176 years deep
It's safe to believe now because after all this time we see change
So rejoice at a milestone on this day
November 4, 2008 forever embedded a place in history
The day we went from all our misery to taking center stage
Writing another Black American Chapter Novel titled "Tears of Joy, Triumphant Laughter."
Ladies and Gentlemen our 44th and first African American President
Barrack Hussein Obama!!!!

Ms. Flashing Lights..

Maybe I was consumed by the flashing lights or
Maybe I had one too many drinks that particular night but, I swore this lady was destined to be my wife
Her scent of a feminine addiction, had me addicted
Forcing my hand to want to be in her life not knowing I would be spending late nights looking for her sight
Get a call from my man like Yo! I see shawty with him
Yet her girls on the other line saying that uh uh boo boo he be hating cuz she with them
Let me talk to her then, She busy right now in the bathroom dang
Mischievous diva's I believe'em, plus my lady is bad and since high school my man been on get back
Cheerleader turned prom queen, Sista dissed him but, I hit that
Damn though girls gone be girls look out for each other but, I done caught them out there a time or two before
Chief Superhoe form the Everydayhoe tribe see she got Indian in her blood not Cherokee but, on the pole showing cheek every 5th day of the week
So my dilemma is who do I believe?
My man..well he full of greed, a fake P.I.M.P living for the PUSSY, Her girls lie
Maybe I should've known from the chocolate covered cherries tatted on her thigh and the one on her lower back saying throwback ass
Maybe it should've been the butterfly wings that appear to fly when her cheeks clap
Either way it was the flashing lights that consumed me that night, too many drinks
Thought shawty was supposed to be my wife yet She can't separate me from her other life
I fell in love with a stripper and she everybody's girl.

A Thugs Prayer

Lord Jesus it is you that keeps me safe in these streets at night and allow me to awaken in the morning.
Lord it is your love that keeps my mind sane and my body healthy. Father God it is you that I turn to when there's no one else there to help me.
I asked you for food and you fed me. I asked you for water and shelter and it is you that quenches my thirst and gives me a place to rest my head.
You bless me with a talent and merely ask me to use it. The lines I write I compose with you in my conscious telling me "don't abuse it."
Yet my decisions for right and wrong I seem to confuse it.
For the things I've done I know that I do not deserve your blessings but, you give them anyway.
 I know that often their times that I sway but, that's why I pray.
 It is only through your guidance that I will make it to heaven someday. Lord you are my light and the Devil well he is my darkness.
It is you lord I lean on to keep me safe in this life prison because temptation is "muthafucker." And you know this that is why you are forgiving.
 I can not make it alone lord I need your help. I alone am weak but, you Lord make me stronger offering your strength so I open up to you and fall to knees and pray to see the light of another day.
AMEN!!!!

Humble Me....

God
I come to you humble with an open mind and in peace
To ask your guidance on the evils that haunt me
These ghost lord make it hard for me to sleep
Makes my state of mind that of a lost soul seeking justice for my grief
Seems funny to me that in a country where to a flag we speak in terms of allegiance and peace
That we destroy other countries for our own financial gain
So much money spent on destruction that now as a overpopulated government slave with a mistake they won't stop bothering me...
Lord I ask you to calm me
They changed my slight happiness into frustration and pain
Took my sunshine away' and they replaced it with black clouds full of rain
Take me away 160 days from the one thing that gives me peace helps me coat with my many pains, Lord I lift my spirit to you in hopes you will guide me
Only you can extinguish this satanic fire that burns deep inside of me
Only you Lord can guide me to a higher ground
It is you that I owe that fact that a poor, lonely lost boy has become a man found
It's your love Lord that keeps me strong so that I don't fall down
With this said and my heart and conscious clear now
I bow down to you on one knee, hands raised in a state of praise
And ask you Lord to Humble Me?

Definition Of A Woman

What is A Women? By definition a women is a female adult person……That's all, That's its but, nah A women is much more than just that…
Women are Jewels, much stronger than diamonds, worth more than iced out platinum, and more precious than pearls…..
Educated as girls to be diverse….Queens of the universe….
Think about it man!!!
Their Sexual presence sparks our essence to be of the opposite gender, as you watch them strut that tender, curved figure…..You realize that they are bigger possessing class to go along with that Ass….intellect to top of those firm breast…sparking conversation that shows you a focused mind on what she wants to do in life….
Now no doubt some are trife, and live that life but, the women I speak of right here and now are those that are hardly found…
The ones you wanna make your wife…not perfect, but worth it…..
The fights, meanliness in due time their just giving you a piece of their mind..
They should have a little attitude….After All they have had to prove themselves for years….battle fears, and even shed some tears from the pain they sustained…Hell nah, man I'm not some type of clown. I'm just speaking the truth as I see it, and paying my respects….Shit, I like'em undressed and wet just like you…hell, I even dogged out a few, that I called my boo…
I don't feel that I'm better than you. I just some time to realize the truth and state the facts instead, of being the average black male trying to mack as a matter of fact, I'm laying it down from the heart cause man you gotta love'em I'm just giving out my……
DEFINITION OF A WOMAN…..

Grown Man (The Growth)

I remember I use to run in and out of the lives of women
I was Mr. Hit and quit it
Don't call me; I'll call you if I'm ever again interested
Then I ran into you beautiful
Tired of the games, wanted to change my ways so you gave me a little freedom allowed me to grow
Showed me the ropes in this thing called love
Funny how as many broads as I was with before
I never had a real kiss or hug nor knew anything about the electricity of sexual bliss
However, I was raised by old school playas and always did that romantic shit
You help me realize it was for all the wrong reasons
I couldn't trust women you help me to exorcise those demons
I was a cold brother that never had any feelings
Shit, truth is I'd leave a bitch alone just because of the season
Fall, winter, spring and summer
I was trying to do Wilt Chamberlain numbers
Then in you the perfect woman comes along and I look beyond your physical features
Break down my barriers and give you a piece of mind, listen to your reason, love you all year no matter the season. First woman in a while that I just lived for your smile, I was even there to wipe the tears from your eyes when you cry, without hesitation I gave you my heart and stripped away my boyish pride. Firmly hold your hand as I look deeply into your eyes to say "I Love You" Thank you for being there from my transformation from a boy into a "Grown Ass Man"

Heard it all before (A man's plea)..

Constantly bothered by the fact that you're no longer holding me
So I call, block my number on the caller ID.
No answer still I guess you know that it's me
Baby, I just want to apologize
Ask for a second chance for the third time
I know I made mistakes in the past
I'm guilty of committing love crimes
I've hit other bitches off with soft lines in their so caramel sweet
but, boo you gotta believe those broads meant nothing just a physical attraction to me
See it's with you that I invest my heart, soul, and mind
I miss you so much; take me back
I promise to change this time
I'll keep the freak inside only giving it to you and promise to love you more
I'll get therapy for my animal instincts
Running up in every whores open door
I'll do anything just this one last time please forgive me
Baby let's get together and go to church on Sunday have the pastor pray for me
Because my flesh is so weak. You see I'm not there when it happens it's my ego and dick that cheat. I don't want to lose out on the best thing I've ever had
Without you I'm incomplete baby please understand
Don't walk away from me holding the next man's hand
Baby, Baby please DAMN!!!

Heard It All Before (Male version)

I'm starting to get this feeling that something's going on
You be out with your girls and that's cool but, baby you late coming home
Before you flip out and get all hostile I realize you grown boo and no I don't have you on no curfew on you.
I just want you to place on my shoes boo
What if it were the other way around?
Be courteous towards my feelings to
See the club closes at two but, you popping in here around six
I understand breakfast at the IHOP or Waffle House but, I think that you're out chasing hard dicks
Now I could be wrong and just jumping to conclusions
Or maybe my Patna seeing you and your friends hop in some brothers rimed up Benz was just and illusion
Yeah he called me this morning
That's why I'm up
Gave me the 411 on where you were parked
I started to get up and let them guns spark; got to the front door and my conscious said stop
Don't look shocked baby pick your jaw up
I'm going to treat this situation like court
Defend yourself give me an alibi, an excuse
I know you got one so talk
Listen boo stop talking with all that attitude we're not outside so use your inside voice
Oh your girl got to drunk and you wanted to make sure she made it home
So you caught a cab ride just so happen to be a candy painted Benz on 20 inch chrome
So why wouldn't you pick up the phone? Scratch that Why wasn't the phone even on?

Oh your battery was dead
Damn I find that kind of hard to believe
Because before you left the phone had a full charge
Alright baby I trust you I'll play boo boo
Maybe something's wrong with phone battery
Now explain your car
Don't look all surprised baby. You know where it was parked
So why was it in Porsche's yard and she didn't even go with ya'll to the club
I decided to call her up she said she was in the house last night getting spoiled by her love
Why you were out creeping
Cheating with your dumb ass friends that don't even have a man
Misery loves company and you fell in their hands
See I'll never understand where I went wrong but, I tell you one thing this shit won't continue on
See I love too hard to shed tears over a whore ass broad
Who in a relationship fucks a another brother she thinks has a lil more paper or because she sees him in a nice car
So see you can't love me then fuck another
Have me on Jerry or Ricki ten years for now because you are the baby mother of another brother
Pack your bags baby girl, I'm through, I caught you This shit is over.

Through My Eyes

It's dark as hell and even with the lights on I can't see through this madness.
Through my window I can hear the children playing but, they seem to do this in an attempt to conceal their sadness.
 In reality, all the laughing simply disguises life's true concerns.
Now the World turns therefore, time evolves and in the process, we slowly dissolve into our original earthly form and all of this is just to be reborn?
Now that's the question we attend classes but, do we really receive lessons or is it a blessing that we can survive in this cold world polluted with guns and drugs.
Do you fall in love?
Or is it that we fall within the threshold thoughts of future loneliness.
I know that to some this makes no sense but, if you go to your window and close your eyes placing your mind in deep thought and actually question reality and imagination you will soon realize it not at all fictious.

Spoken Word.....

You ask when I speak, who do I speak for?
See my spoken words are from the heart so I speak for
Those dysfunctional families that have been torn apart by drugs, sex, and violence
I speak for those misguided minors that are lost in the ghettos hoping someone will find them
For those locked behind bars with the right to remain silent
I speak for those that choose not to speak
If you are one of those folks that refuse to hear me, then I won't speak but,
Write my lines in Braille and make you feel me
I speak on and off beat, I speak to and for the streets
Speak for those 9 to 5 brothers and those that choose to the street hustle and handle heat
That's who I speak for
I speak for those soldiers at war with other nations, I speak for my ancestors before me that were hung from plantations
I speak in terms of violence, I speak in terms of peace
I speak for those innocent children who are fathered by the streets
I speak for those single mothers that struggle to hold their feet
Stay strong baby girl I feel your grief
See my words are a personal war an ongoing beef
I speak pleasure, I speak pain, Speak politics and sex
What do I speak for?
I speak for what I believe in those powerful words that for some may leave your eardrums bleeding That's what I speak for Spoken word

Dear You

If I had a wish
Lady I'd wish he'd never left you feeling like this because I can feel your pain
So at times I find myself holding my head in shame because I played a silly game but, with you it was to win
It was just that complicated situations I was left facing attempting to read your faces and decided to let you go rather than chase you and attempt to persuade you that I was placed here on earth for you
That we were meant to be and Us, Our relationship a blind destiny
Shit, I don't know about you but the feeling of your body next to mine was supreme Ecstasy
Something so close to heavenly that it brought the real man out of me.
I know you said you didn't think then that I would grow to be the man that I am now and to let go of the past but, those 4-page letters are epic
Feeling expresses through pen and pad to learn one another better not to mention the thoughts were so sweet.
Reading your written lines as in my mind I could hear you speak.
Psst, remember that night on the beach
The things you said to me
The feeling that overcame you the moment you released.
Unfortunately, the situation was always her, him, she and me
I was hurting when I found out that it was him not me and that you really did it
Confused, thought I lost you so I committed
Praying that the foundation you laid down was naked and strong so the relationship would become and unbreakable bond
Damn! The mood switched
Fuck!!!! I should have waited kept a little more patience told you the raw truth damn if you may have thought I was hating

Yet at the time my luck wasn't too good plus you molded me
Help me open my eyes to what true love was
Such a sweet heart, a beautiful princess
My stomach clutches when I begin reminiscing
Cocaine passion, SugarCaine heart
My most complicated love story although together seems to have missing parts
Such a passionate art

Inspired by The Orgasm

Alphabet Love....

Aaagh…Heavy **B**reathing from achieving the ultimate **C**limax; Let you witness the **D**own south experience got my tongue game down pact. **E**bony erotica is what we can call this experience all day **F**oreplay. Leading to sunrise **G**oodbyes, Hypothetically speaking on Karma Sutra's **H**idden positions. So we'll **I**mprovise break out a few toys and gadgets. Your love **J**uices are flowing from the double finger rub clitoral stimulation while engaged in caramel **K**isses. **L**ay your body down; lure me into position, passionate **M**oans released, let's me know I'm where you want me to be. **N**ine inches deep, hold the **O** in my name while rubbing my back, smack my ass a lil I'm a freak like dat. Then switch positions, body shifted arch your back slightly enough to get it. Now my perfectly placed stroke of **P**erfection has you reaching your sexual peak almost there where? Ecstasy. Your pleasure is shown by the way your legs **Q**uivering. This is your private fantasy remember, you wanted to **R**ide me on the love swing define the meaning of a true **S**tallion to me. Body frictions arousing a tingling **T**emptation. **U**ghh I'm in love with the sex faces. **V**olcanic eruptions, an orgasmic **W**etness unexplainable, **X** rated sex yet a few X's unattainable. Like your leg on the pool table, me stroking from the back. You watching me, demanding more, answering every question I ask with a **Y**es. Then we both fall fast asleep you collapse on my chest you catch some **Z**'s then awakened by the wink of sunrise. It's Morning….

Let's talk about Sex...

Let's talk about my body naked and hard
Your body naked and wet
Let's talk about me placing kisses on your neck
How about adding some romance let's get some candles lit
Feel that tight grip of my hands around your waist
Is it just me or do you get those anxious butterfly like feeling, as on a bed of roses we lay
Eye contact just seconds before we kiss
Or that feeling that you get just as my tongue begins to hit those secret spots that increase anticipation
"Calm down" I whisper as my tongue caresses your breast and nipples I can feel your heartbeat racing
Let's talk about how I get those sexy faces as I slide to your navel
Or how as I go low I tease your clit with a soft blow
Tracing your body down to your toes
Let's talk about that shiver as I roll you over and massage oils into your back
And that feeling you get when I strategically place a kiss on the back of your thigh
You scream "please stop teasing me"
So in doggie style position I place my tongue in between your thighs, lay on my back, again I tightly grab your waist then position you and allow you the honor to sit on my face
As a tear slips your eye; Now let's talk about penetration
Inch by inch I take it slow until I fully submerge my nature inside of your love river,
Different positions lead to different destinations. My goal is to have your body shaking and I'm gentleman you cum first, play hard to get I put in hard work. It's your body I'm craving that candy precipitation that leaves your hands clutching the sheets, hips raising like fuck is doing to me
My answer those deep stokes of penetration, chasing your orgasm
Now let's talk about that Climax you know the tingling sensation.
Sunrise I'm up early breakfast is awaiting Thank you lady...

Love Experience

See Mi Lady I don't just want you to experience pleasure but, take you to the paradigm of orgasm
Dive so deep inside your love that your body spasms
Nah, bedroom booms are not enough for you; What you want is a mandingo backstroke that makes the Earth appear to shatter
A man not afraid to fulfill your freaky inhibitions
So face to face with your sugarwalls I indulge in a tongue kiss
Up, down, side to side slow acute and wide circles
I'll pretend your clique is a straw and suck then swallow all of your love
Only to give it back with seductive, intimate well place kisses
in those secret places I found while exploring your skin with my tongues caress
Take a bite of that apple bottom ass; As I crawl up your back and enter you
Slow, deep and hard
Grip the sheets, bite the pillow…Oh My God, you mutha
Talking half words like we suffer from a speech impediment Now all jokes aside this moment right here is the type of sex that'll get you pregnant!!!
Tried to keep this secret but now the neighbors know both our names and the they jealous cause the cops come knocking telling us that we're disturbing the peace when we are just two freaks trying to get a piece…And simply planned to fall fast asleep until morning…..

Director...Starring You

OOO!
I had a vision that the sex would be unbelievable
Then you had that talk like your sexual chemistry was an addiction that would leave me to needing you, Constantly licking my lips after eating tasting your liquid love
A warm, sweet succulent reminder of a cinnabon
I ask you to pick your favorite position
Slowly, and deeply my hard love enters your passion walls
Your legs sprawl, mid way through the first stroke we both call for the lord
My stroke is in sync with your bodies rhythm as we make seductive eye contact
I ask "Do you like that?"
Before I get a response back I nipple on your ear, kiss on your neck and collarbone
This is my attempt to further turn you on!
Our words are exotic moans, we're speaking that sex language
Every other word is four letters; and your body is dangerous
Giving me that tingling sensation, dick drench from slippery penetration
You don't have to speak your sex face says it....
Together we're almost home when I stop giving you the dick, slide out
Take your creamy wet love and place it back into my mouth while I turn you over
Lights, camera, action take two scene one is over......
Now you throw it like at me like a quarterback
I don't know how to act; Intense sexual impact
SEX is like crack and I'm your number one fiend
Right now, doesn't matter you can tell me anything
I swear I can hear birds chirping while swimming in your ocean

I thought you were from the west coast, one leg up in three-wheel motion
I'm losing focus you look back and notice you got me as I watch in amazement
Turned on by your faces; I dig deep and find new inspiration…. before gotta hold on
Gently slap your ass, then I grab your waist and hold on
As you bodies movements take me into out of space
All I can see is…..blind erections, your bodies perfection is and you possess the perfect sexual weapon. I place your leg on my leg to give me leverage
For deep, hard submerged introductions to your love muscle
Almost there I swear, holding back so bad that it' numbing my leg
How about to take me for a ride. Place my joystick inside and play your favorite game
Almost out of my brain, this love is insane
About to pop a vein holding on for dear life
Damn babe you nice but, I got one surprise left for you though
See I don't wanna cum like that. SIT ON MY FACE, Nah not like that it's just to easy
Let me taste you, You can watch me or stroke my hard manhood
It's your decision, stop pretending you're not as freaky as me
Cum for the D!, I need you to cum for me! I got the same energy
Your flavor is enough to make me….agrhh!!! Shit baby
Now lay here on my chest and go to sleep.
Breakfast is on me….in bed when you awaken…

Everyday Memory

When Last I saw her she lay there
Naked and shaking
From the precise penetration
Stimulating her G spot
Body provoked into convulsions; Neighbor's banging on the wall from all the sexual commotion
See it started I was making groceries had a list and forgot it because shawty had her body on notice
Scent of woman that had brothers open; Focused on the way she moves in those Jimmy Choo shoes
Dudes seeing interludes of her and him in the nude
Butt Naked!
I had a secret though
My tongue is a secret weapon
Your Clit, I'll caress it while using something in your toy collection
The coexistence is so serious
Climbing the walls, driving you delirious
Switch Now I use a bullet to caress the clit, while my tongue searches your sugar walls
For that spot that gives you a tickling sensation while we playing the alphabet game
You know I move my tongue in certain ways and you guess what letter it is, often times resulting in me spelling your name.
The love scene was insane

An Everyday Memory......

Regular sex..
This is not regular sex, this session should be epic....
My goal is to give u multiple orgasms; my tongue caressing your creamy center looking for proactive treasures, Teach me how to arouse your intimate pleasures
I listen well, and I need an A for effort, I'm a good student
My lips kissing your apple booty
I whisper to you what can I do better? Eat your ass for extra credit.
Fuck it if it was nasty, you taste like a vegan sweetness.
Have you ever been catered to, told that the sex is 100 percent about you.....
Cum first, what's your favorite angle, back shots, sideview, or missionary.
We can do frog to if that's your choice Its want you want
A Sexual genie with unlimited wishes, Simply want to release those innermost inhibitions
Something different like….
Applying wet Kisses while jerking off, Your essence on the tip of tongue in the literal sense
I want you on my face, I'll hold your waist
Your ass is suicidal, smother me in your creamy lake
This is that top of line sex , That shit so good you feel like you gotta pay for it
That no matter the time juice and breakfast type sex
That fuck yo man, call her sunshine we ain't never going back to where we belong Forbidden sex
We not suppose to have it, It's different. My clear vision is legs in a V to the ceiling, giving you sexual healing till you catch that convulsion feeling, Nigga get off
That hold my head in between your legs, head back eyes roll making you cum
This sex is different , Not regular sex, nah this is something epic
We connect

Orgasm

Glad that Tank set the ambience for this
Me, you burning candles..conversation such a stimulus
I wanted to create a masterpiece and his vocals are the added effects
You have the starring role, credited as co-writer and creator
A Vivid imagination, This is hand crafted
The painting we title it orgasm and its been sometime creating but a genius mind takes time to design
Our words are the brush strokes chemically crafting the passion
Our touch created by the dopamine of our verses
Her kisses make me nervous; performance anxiety
Though through them and her eyes I can find my place
Tongue begins to trace her curves in search of her paradise
Intimate pleasures and favors returned Toes begin to curl, sheets wrinkle from the fist clinching
Pick your position no words needed, as it is my pleasure to dive into your depths
Its strategic I know your desires and your body tells me how to deliver the dictation
I listen well and like to believe I'm a great notetaker
Her legs in a V, me using both obtuse and acute angles to deliver her the deepest satisfaction
We are creating an interlude to a fuck action mixtape
Her words become serotonin driven as atop my face she finds her rhythm
My face between waist outlining her feminine features, she diets well she taste so delicious
Orgasm the climax of sexual excitement, characterized by intensely pleasurable feelings
Painted by US!!!

Cunnilingus

I caress your clit in cursive
She deeply falls in love with my verses.
Her favorites words are now adjectives and verbs, lord have mercy cunnilingus!
I am a sexual linguist
We be speaking in tongues, tracing her curves this is all the prerequisite to get what she deserves
Deep dick and ass smacking however, I would rather signature first.
Toes curl while you cum from Cunnilingus.
A loose tongue, you run, then freeze while you cum
Nugga, see how you do I can't move! "I love and hate you"
I use my mouth is a tool, it crawls up and down your stimulus package, crafted for your pleasure I'm not the type who taste you simply to achieve wetness for penetration
Nah, as a cunnilingus I want you to achieve multiple orgasms, squirt if you must…I'll swallow your juices.
The sweet Appleberry bliss that pleasures my lips as I can't stop.
Won't stop performing interludes of cunnilingus.
Tongue up and down, tempting, teasing your clit round and round circular rotations; did I mention I will meet your toy half way.
Vibrate from the top, my tongue sucks the lower portions.
Apply a gentle pleasure with hopes of you fulfilling one promise
An orgasm on my palette.
Cunnilingus!

About Last Night....

The sexual session was epic
It stemmed from the patience, and conversation about life lessons
A verbal masturbation that led to deep Penetration from different positions
Freestyles, as this night wasn't written
We only went off the feeling and yes it was a vibe.
Looking into your eyes as you ride
My tongue service in electric rhythms searching for orgasm
There she is that uncontrolled body spasm of her blank canvas
Now stimulated and recreated with verbs, nouns and adjectives
A description of a virtual rendezvous
We have arrived at a place where passion lies, and fantasies fulfilled
That place where imagination feels real.
Her warm chocolate connects with orgasmic strokes and French kiss
Mind blowing conversation about in common nostalgia
There were Delicious memories created in last nights moments
About last night

The Session

I'm trying to recreate the moment
In my mind visualize her imagery
How I explored her body; tongue tracing her perfect symmetry.
I planned for her to remember me
Take her body to the edge of ecstasy and have her wait for me there
Don't cum alone, cum with me
Let's make beautiful music together
Our bodies and vocals combined sound like a symphony
Our chemistry, we connected through stimulated conversations; mentally masturbating while asking how her day went
Her skin is a cognac color, so I must be a coke blend
And brown liquor well it keeps my blood flowing to erotic regions
She's told me before she likes that deep shit so
I descended to her love canal in search of subconscious thoughts, she likes me there
Passionate stares, our eyes questioning each motion like how did you get here; mouth using profane language like you muthafucka! Damn!
Ass slapping; back scratching; fist clutching sheets and climaxing
Fuck Action! like them old mixtapes where they chopped and screwed the session
Morning sun, juice and breakfast. Both half naked; indulging in the essence of the other
These are the unspoken lessons; that force thought provoking questions
The sessions!!

The Head Doctor (For the Fellas)

Oh shit Ma,
That feeling is so astonishing
I'm confused can't figure out what's better
Is it the warm wetness of your mouth or that slurping sound you make?
Shit, you got a brother gone in the head
You deliver a College level Education now studying pre-med
Graduated Magna Cum Lata of your class
You bobbing up and down; wireless connection using no hands
My toes curling; leg straight up in the air
Your vocals are so sweet you should've been signed along time ago but, the lucky signature was me. Head game is crazy; perform pornographic feats that can only amaze me
You take me in so deep making my knees buckle
Let me sit up on the edge of the bed and watch you perform
Beat bumping, head bobbing as you record platinum songs at the same time giving me a round of applause. Must have been studying real well cause ma delivery is without flaws
Sliding up and down every inch while your tongue is massaging my balls
Feels like you are almost breaking the law and a nigga should've signed a clause stating that you're not responsible for him losing self-control
I can't hold on any longer
You're sucking on my lollipop like it's fulfilling your hunger
That warm, wet sensation got me making strange faces, feeling a tingling sensation as your head I'm embracing……
Ma got me shaking like a cardiac patient until I reach climax
Then my dick becomes a straw and she swallows me like I'm her favorite drink
WOW!!! Professional, well-educated lady should've put that on tape.

Tongue n the panties

Can't wait to dive head first between your legs into your emotions and taste it
Shit, you don't even have to return the favor
Delicious flavor I savior like a grape now-later
Your love juices are of a cranberry flavor
Hmmm, my favorite
Place to be is in between your legs naked
These moments I'm craving
Enjoying those alluring sex faces, Sensual voices you're making
While you're enjoying the sight of me masturbating my manhood
Daytime salivation, looking at my watch
Patiently waiting for the upcoming sexual stimulation
I'm a freak and wanting to take you places
Placing my Tongue in the panties is part of my nature.
Taste I savior and it left you shaking.

Teasing me...

You wanted to use your body as inspiration by teasing me
Your body speaks a sex language; Them curves dangerous
Watching you is a sight of shear amazement
She can't be real
Mentally I'm picturing you naked
I use my tongue as if I'm going through mazes
Taking you places, through clitoral stimulation
Look at you now baby…eyes all hazy, exotic moans and complimented sex faces
Legs shaking; from the orgasmic vibrations leaving your body
Eyes saying you want me to penetrate your wetness, guide me slowly
Stroking my manhood as if you know it's your saving glory
You ain't had it this good in a minute
Before placing me in the center
You decide to make love to me with the wetness of your mouth
69 ways to a love scene is what I'm about, so I travel once again down south and find out why
That tattoo says that you are a peach. The taste is so sweet; it speaks to me
Your body is a sexual artistry
Now submerged, splash you become wetter by the stroke
Together our music is the perfect note
You got my hard love on swole; can't envision ever letting go
Harder and deeper you ask; Call me genie man
Your wish is my command
Loving that beautiful nature and next time you talk with her tell your mom I said thank you
Roll you over face-down; I slightly raise your leg
While you arch your back
Then I slide in slowly; hold it there for me

I rest inside your walls for a second letting you feel each and every inch of my measurement
So that you know it's me
Then slide all the way out
Tongue goings crazy over the vision so I place your love back in my mouth
Before re-entry take the head of my dick; massage your clit
This feeling is ridiculous so wet didn't even know I could make it cum like that
I'm holding back I need this moment to last
You mount me reverse cowgirl knowing I love to watch that chocolate ass
You're so, so thick…shit! Go get'em cowgirl
Thoroughbred; get your ride on girl
My legs lock; there goes that tingling feeling
Awaken from my daydream
Sticky jeans; what a memory

Sexual Voodoo

Damn Baby,
Why do I think of you the way that I do
Subjecting myself to blind visions……Subleminal intentions of me and you in sexual positons
Intensely spurgin' as I'm submerging within da depths of your ocean……raising your deepest, most intimate emotions
Baby, I'm thinking devotion but, it's really just the blind xctasy of dat sweet-ass fragrance you wear…Seduction of my mind,body and soul wit dat bedroom stare…..Forcin' me to pursue….thoughts that's long overdue
As I continue in search of open chances….to make sexual advances involved in exotic dances
Caressing your sculptured figure….Tell me one thing baby
Can I be your nigga?…Shit I'd settle for just being your slave
Ablige your every want and need cause your love is what I crave
Maybe it's just yo body,voice or the way you do the things that you do but, whatever it is girl I'm obsessed by you….

Explicit Nature

We hit the house, enroute to the bedroom we detour to the couch
We're mouth to mouth
Until each other we undress quiet whispers in your ear
Both of us have had a long day at work let's relieve some of that stress
Then there's other places on your body that my lips press
Next, my tongue taste your clit, your mouth strokes my dick
No hands; you want me to see your real skills.
OKAY! I'm impressed. As I slap your ass, down my chest you slide
You place my hard love inside your love waterfall and seductively whisper for me to "hold on for this ride…"
Trying not to lose control I place my hands on your hips
Using my perfect grip I turn you over on your side; lift your leg at a 45 degree angle then slide inside then I apply those long, deep strokes then I turn you again.
Face to face, slide down use my tongue once again then slowly I penetrate, my hand in your hand pinned downed to the bed you bite your bottom lip giving me that sexy face.
About to reach that place I turn you over once again that's when you start to take over turns me on the way that ass is bouncing
Slap both cheeks then slowly spread them so that I can get that much deeper
We're so excited mouths wipe open but, there's no screaming
Both of us giving one another that orgasmic cream
Awaken the next morning pinching one another assuring ourselves that it wasn't all a dream.

XXXPlictly You....

It's the middle of the night and our bodies are conversating
The way you've been moving on me has got me stimulated
Patiently waiting till that moment of penetration. My goal is to have your body quivering and shaking from the love we're making
The moment when I insert my hard passion into your love canal
Lay your body down as I slow the tempo down, Tracing each and every curve with my tongue
Whispering in your ear your name as I climb inside
The head of my dick teasing your clit as my tongue gently caresses your breast
Eye contact, and the feeling of my flesh against yours forces you to scream out yes
Barely asked the question yet, would you mi....
So I go down, Using my tongue now to caress each and every part of your love fruit and tasting it's sweet erotic juice
Eyes wide; Amazed by your birthday suit trying to be patient heavily breathing can't wait to enter you. Splash, is the sound as I enter your love canal with my joystick
Now control this, make me do what it takes to please you whether missionary, sideways, from behind or you can ride. Feeling inside your passage is unexplainable must be close to heaven because I think I see angels. Your eyes closed it's evident, trying to moan but, my deep strong stroke has you speechless, In exctasy our words are lost
Allowing you to cum first, then I follow shortly behind
Climax, both of us shivering, body still quivering from the deliverance of that sexual experience
I lye there next to you; your body attached to mine
What I tried to say earlier was would you mind if I blow your mind?

www.ingramcontent.com/pod-product-compliance
Lightning Source LLC
Chambersburg PA
CBHW021022090426
42738CB00007B/865